NATIONAL SECURITY AGENCY
Ft. George G. Meade, MD

18 October 2007

Systems and Network Analysis Center

<u>Best Practices for Storage Networks</u>

This document
contains 30 sheets.

Table of Contents

1. Executive Summary

Storage networks often contain company proprietary information, trade secrets, and mission critical data. Ensuring the availability of the storage network and its components as well as the confidentiality and integrity of information in transit and at rest within the storage network is vital to the success of the company. Implementing the common best practices described in this paper will provide greater information assurance for the storage architecture and data within the storage network.

This paper will present general storage network security best practices followed by specific best practices for Network Attached Storage (NAS), Storage Area Networks (SAN), and Internet Small Computer Systems Interface (iSCSI) storage networks. Included are security mechanisms that should be used to protect the content and function of storage networks. Techniques that employ these mechanisms will protect the components, interfaces, and protocols in storage networks and will provide fewer opportunities for attack. Sample architectures that incorporate many of the security features are also provided.

2. General Storage Network Security

A storage network can take one of three main forms: Network Attached Storage (NAS), a Storage Area Network (SAN), or an Internet Small Computer Systems Interface (iSCSI) storage network. Each form of storage network may be protected using best practices that require the use of various security mechanisms. A security mechanism is broadly defined to be anything that provides at least a minimal amount of security to either a network component or the network itself. Security mechanisms might be security protocols, configuration options, or even network components themselves. Security mechanisms provide varying degrees of security depending on their function and their placement in the network architecture. They might be used to provide access control, or to prevent data corruption or redirection.

This paper will provide current best practices that should be included in secure storage networks.

Refer to Appendix 1 for a list of acronyms used throughout the document. Refer to Appendix 2 for a summary of general best practices for storage networks and the types of security services each best practice provides. Refer to Appendices 3, 4, and 5 for a summary of the best practices for NAS, SAN, and iSCSI networks, respectively. Refer to Appendix 6 for a list of references.

2.1 Physical Security, Operations Security, and Business Continuity Planning

Certain best practices are common to securing any storage networking environment. These include physical security, operations security (OPSEC), and business continuity planning. Strong physical security measures should be implemented, since this is the first line of defense. Data availability, integrity, and confidentiality are all at great risk without appropriate physical security. Simply using a password as an access control mechanism is not a complete safeguard against unauthorized entry if there is weak physical security. Access to a physical port on a device can provide the attacker the opportunity to bypass, terminate, or steal secure logins to the storage network by taking advantage of faults or flaws in the implementation of access control mechanisms. Unused ports (both logical and physical) and unused protocols should be disabled on all storage network devices and management workstations.

Likewise, best practices for maintaining OPSEC should be implemented. All aspects of operations should be controlled, including hardware, software, firmware, media, and personnel. Procedures should detail all operations, and extra care should be taken when media containing sensitive business data is physically transported. Headline news continues to relate stories of theft or loss of huge quantities of data containing personal and confidential information. Proper OPSEC would help mitigate these vulnerabilities.

It is important to have a business continuity plan so that a disaster will not completely destroy the business. The plan might include provisions for data replication to a disaster recovery site. Backup copies of device operating systems, configurations, application software and data should be securely maintained both locally and off site for disaster recovery purposes.

2.2 Documentation and Planning

Implementing secure storage networks requires proper documentation and planning. Documentation should be generated that includes hardware and software inventories, storage network topology diagrams, policy, and procedures. Security should be a focus throughout the documentation, and access to the documentation should be controlled and logged. Documentation should not be limited to automatically generated storage network topology diagrams stored within software, but should also include periodically updated hardcopies that are accessible on demand by authorized personnel. A risk analysis should be performed before deploying or integrating new storage architectures, and existing storage architectures should be re-analyzed before making any modifications. The outcome should include a determination of required protection levels for all data and devices in the architecture. A storage security policy should be maintained and incorporated into the larger enterprise security policy. Procedures should be documented in detail and available to the appropriate personnel. The storage network topology and how it fits in to the enterprise architecture should be documented, maintained, and stored in a secure location.

The Common Criteria Evaluation Assurance Levels (EAL) and Federal Information Processing Standards (FIPS) provide different levels of security assurance. The greatest security benefits can be provided by components that have achieved the highest levels of certification, so these should be incorporated into the storage network architecture.

2.3 Availability and Confidentiality

It is important to implement common best practices that provide assurance of availability and confidentiality. Uninterruptible Power Supply (UPS) should be used for all components in the architecture. Remove single points of failure within the architecture by adding redundancy and failover mechanisms. Data should be backed up appropriately to portable media and stored at a secure, off-site location.

Strong encryption should be implemented throughout the storage architecture, both in the storage network and in the management network. Encrypt communications between management stations and storage network devices. The strongest hash/encryption algorithms supported by the NAS device and clients should be used. For example, Secure Hash Algorithm 256 (SHA-256) is stronger than Message Digest 5 (MD5) and Advanced Encryption Standard (AES) is stronger than DES, therefore SHA-256 and AES should be used if possible.

2.4 Network Management and Access Control

A number of network management and access control best practices should be implemented. Network devices typically offer two options for device configuration and management: local administration via a serial connection, or remotely via an Ethernet connection. Perform device management locally, exclusively via the console port, since this is the most secure form of management. If the devices must be managed remotely, perform out-of-band (OOB) management and only use protocols that incorporate strong encryption (i.e. current, patched versions of SSH or SSL). The OOB management network should not be connected to any other network, including the Internet. A less secure remote management option would be in-band management using only protocols that incorporate strong encryption. Regardless of remote management type (i.e. in-band or OOB), storage network administrative access should be restricted via access control lists to a minimal set of Internet Protocol (IP) addresses if possible. Insecure protocols such as TELNET, FTP, RSH, and HTTP should be disabled. A modem should never be connected to the serial port for remote management.

Access control lists should restrict any Simple Network Management Protocol (SNMP) traffic sent from unauthorized devices. SNMP version 3 (SNMPv3) should be used rather than SNMPv1 or SNMPv2. SNMP communications should be logged.

All management passwords and SNMP community strings should comply with strong rules set forth in policy. Administrators should use unique passwords, should regularly change their passwords in accordance with password expiration policy, and should not reuse old passwords. Always change device default passwords before connecting to an operational or management network. Two or more-factor authentication should be required for administrators of each of the components in the storage network.

Use Role-Based Access Control (RBAC) if it is available to manage storage network devices. RBAC provides much granularity in defining different administrative operations and associating these operations with different administrators. Administrators will only be able to perform those operations required to satisfy their job responsibilities.

Access Control mechanisms should record login failures. Perform periodic audits to look for patterns of failed login events, since this might be evidence of attempted unauthorized access.

Another best practice for access control is to close all terminal shell windows and log out of the administrative workstation immediately after performing administrative tasks on storage network devices. Also, after using the serial port on a storage network device to manage the device, log out of the device before physically unplugging the cable from the serial port. Following this practice will prevent unauthorized automatic serial port access.

2.5 Layer 2-3 Security

Access to IP storage network devices should be restricted to authorized IP addresses and hostnames. This can be accomplished by using Access Control List (ACL) filters applied to layer 3 network devices such as IP routers. Physical separation or disconnection of networks as well as Virtual Local Area Networks (VLANs) should be used appropriately. Monitoring should also be performed to verify expected network traffic, and to detect unusual and anomalous network traffic. Active and passive techniques should be used. An example of an active technique is conducting a port scan of the network. Examples of passive techniques are running a network sniffer, viewing device log files, and viewing Address Resolution Protocol (ARP) table entries. Switch port security should be enabled on all interfaces of a LAN switch to limit access to only those devices listed as authorized devices. For guidance on securing LAN switches, refer to the "Cisco IOS Switch Security Configuration Guide" available on www.nsa.gov. For guidance on securing IP routers, refer to the "Router Security Configuration Guide" available on www.nsa.gov as well.

2.6 Operating System and Application Security

Best practices for operating system and application security should be followed. It is important to configure the operating system and application software so that it is in the most secure state. Ensure that all applicable devices, including management workstations, are kept current with virus scanner and anti-spyware software updates. Delete unnecessary application programs from systems in the storage architecture. It is possible that some application programs used during development of the product were mistakenly left in the product after sale. These programs can cause problems if later discovered to be accessible by unauthorized operators.

Data security might be compromised if storage network device operating systems include debuggers. An operational storage network device operating system should never contain any debuggers. Steps should be taken to turn off or eliminate any debuggers present to avoid unauthorized reboots, denial of service, and unauthorized modification of data stored on the storage network.

Verify that operating systems and application programs, including storage management applications, have current and stable security patches installed. Check bug tracking web sites regularly, since the quantity of new attacks is increasing and the time it takes for them to be automated and made publicly available is decreasing. If your applications are affected and a patch is unavailable, a decision should be made after performing a risk analysis to continue running unpatched or remove the application from the environment until a patch is available.

On a similar note, only install software and firmware upgrades that have originated from a trusted source and have been verified on a non-production system. Periodically audit the storage network systems to verify that all software, firmware, and patches are at the expected version/release level.

2.7 Attack Detection and Prevention

Mechanisms should be employed to detect and prevent: 1) attacks and 2) unnecessary traffic from entering the storage network. Logs are useful for detecting attacks. Logs should be maintained on all storage network devices and storage network management devices, and analyzed regularly. Logs should be sent to external devices rather than stored locally on the devices creating the logs to help prevent log modification by an attacker. Any abnormal activities in a log such as changes made by administrators at times when the real administrator was not actually present, deleted or appended logs with missing entries, or repeated failed login attempts are indications of potential hacking.

Synchronization of time on network devices is important to detect attacks. Synchronize time on storage network devices using the Network Time Protocol (NTP) for ease of attack correlation and analysis. The NTP server might be located on the Internet or it might be on an internal Local Area Network (LAN). The more secure option is to source time locally OOB.

Two more tools are useful for detecting and preventing attacks: Intrusion Detection Systems (IDS) and firewalls. IDS should be used to detect anomalies and known attacks. IDS can be either network-based (NIDS) or host-based (HIDS). Both should be used when a medium-high degree of assurance of detection is required. IDS should be deployed both on the operational end-user network and on the management network. Firewalls should be used to prevent malicious and unnecessary traffic from entering the storage architecture.

3. Network Attached Storage (NAS) Security

Securing Network Attached Storage (NAS) involves employing Transmission Control Protocol/Internet Protocol (TCP/IP) security mechanisms, as well as employing additional mechanisms that are specific to NAS technologies and protocols. Two major NAS file system protocols exist, Common Internet File System (CIFS) and Network File System (NFS). Some NAS security mechanisms are common to both CIFS and NFS, while others are specific to either CIFS or NFS. The remainder of this section describes the best security practices for NAS.

3.1 Confidentiality and Integrity

Confidentiality and integrity of all data and metadata (i.e. protocol header field information) is a security goal for the NAS environment and may be provided by the NAS device itself or by a third party device. Most NAS devices support IP Security (IPSec) to protect data in transit between a NAS client and a NAS device. Third party encryption devices may be used to protect data at rest. The best practice is to use IPSec encryption (Authentication Header (AH) + Encapsulating Security Payload (ESP)) between a NAS client and a third party encryption device. Also use the strongest available encryption on a third party device to encrypt the data in transit between the third party device and the NAS device as well as the data at rest on the NAS device.

3.2 Network Data Management Protocol (NDMP)

If Network Data Management Protocol (NDMP) is used for network-based NAS backup, authentication should be required. Access control lists should restrict any NDMP traffic sent from unauthorized devices. NDMP communications should be logged.

3.3 Authentication and Access Control

Authentication and access control can be provided via data segmentation. The two major file system protocols, CIFS and NFS, also have applicable authentication and access control mechanisms. These are described in the following sections.

3.3.1 Data Segmentation

Two mechanisms that can be employed to provide access control to data residing on NAS devices are logical segmentation and physical segmentation. A Virtual Filer (vFiler) can be used to provide a low level of access control by logically segmenting a single NAS device into multiple NAS devices, comparable to what a VLAN does to a LAN. Environments that require a high level of access control should use physical segmentation rather than logical segmentation.

Separate NAS devices should be used for each group or level of security classification e.g. one NAS device for unclassified data, a separate NAS device for confidential data, and so on.

3.3.2 CIFS

A NAS device running CIFS can be made more secure by employing New Technology Local Area Network Manager version 2 (NTLMv2) or Kerberos authentication mechanisms. For instance, NTLMv2 should be used for a medium level of authentication assurance, while Kerberos is most appropriate for environments where a high level of authentication assurance is required. Use mutual Kerberos authentication if possible, because it is the authentication of each device to the other, and this is more secure than one-way authentication (i.e. one device authenticates itself to the other device). Weak authentication mechanisms such as LAN Manager (LM) and NTLMv1 should always be disabled on all Windows domain controllers and clients. An IDS should be used to alert on LM and NTLMv1 to detect attempts to authenticate using a weaker form of authentication. If Kerberos is used, alerts should also be generated for NTLMv2 authentication attempts to indicate that NTLMv2 authentication was attempted rather than the stronger Kerberos authentication. Another CIFS NAS best practice is to restrict share permissions to specific users and groups. This provides a form of access control to NAS data.

3.3.3 NFS

A NAS device running NFS can be made more secure by employing Kerberos authentication mechanisms. Use NAS client operating systems that support Kerberos for authentication. Establish privileged user accounts and associate them with specific IP addresses. Log and ignore requests from privileged users at unauthorized IP addresses. When a client makes a request to a NAS device from the "root" account, the device should treat the request as being from the "nobody" account. Use export options appropriately on all NAS devices to help ensure that data is only accessible to devices that are authorized to receive the data. Configure NAS devices to log and ignore "showmount" requests. If responses must be sent, create local hostname aliases and configure exports to those aliases to obscure the information an attacker can enumerate when making "showmount" requests.

3.4 Sample NAS Security Architecture

A sample NAS architecture that implements security mechanisms is shown in Figure 1. Two NAS networks are shown: one classified and one unclassified. End-to-end IPSec encryption is used between the unclassified NAS device and its clients, as well as between the third party encryption device and clients of the classified NAS device. The third party encryption device encrypts data sent to the classified NAS device, and the data remains encrypted while stored on the classified NAS device. Kerberos is used for authentication of NAS clients to NAS devices. The Key Distribution Center (KDC) resides in the Demilitarized Zone (DMZ). Network Intrusion Detection Systems (NIDS) are strategically positioned between the router/firewall device and the Internet and end-user networks. A limited number of protocols are used to communicate with the management network.

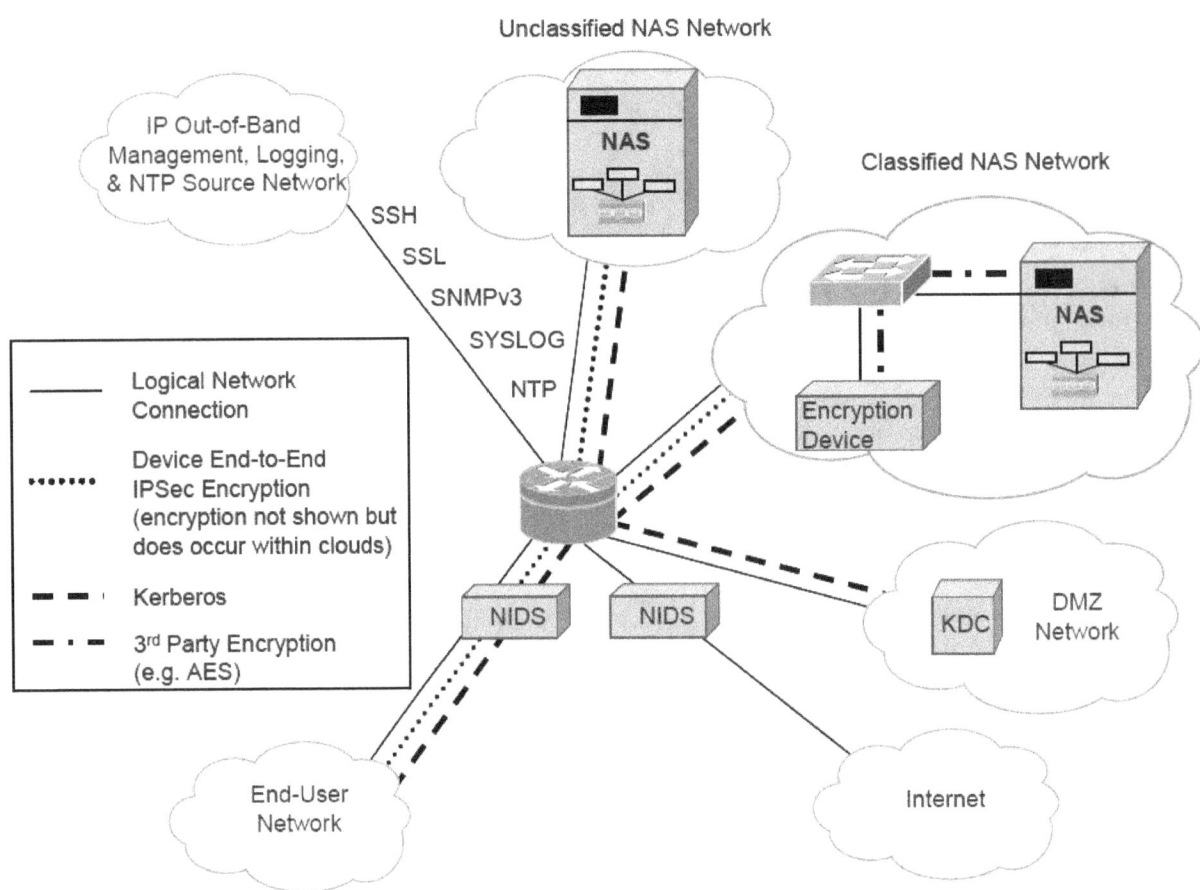

Figure 1: NAS Architecture with Added Security

4. Storage Area Network (SAN) Security

Many options exist for implementing SAN security. A number of SAN-specific security mechanisms should be integrated into the SAN environment to provide confidentiality, authentication, and access control. Following the recommendations outlined in this section will provide a reasonable level of security assurance for SAN architectures.

4.1 Confidentiality

Confidentiality services help guarantee the privacy of data, by using advanced encryption techniques, to ensure only authorized individuals see the information. Confidentiality of data and metadata can be provided with a number of mechanisms. Equipment that supports the Fibre Channel Security Protocols (FC-SP) should be selected and properly configured for use throughout the SAN. FC-SP provides Fibre Channel frame confidentiality through the use of ESP encryption. In addition to FC-SP, encrypt inter-switch communications using a strong cryptographic algorithm. Enable and use protocols that provide strong cryptography for switch administration and management (e.g. SSH, SSL, SNMPv3) to protect network traffic that contains passwords.

Data-at-rest on storage devices such as disks or tapes should be encrypted using a strong cryptographic algorithm. Encryption appliances are commercially available that perform this function. However, typically the encryption device does not encrypt data between the servers and the SAN switches, but rather between the switches and the storage devices. Ideally, encryption would occur at the server so that data is encrypted (i.e. confidentiality is maintained) from server to SAN switch to storage device (i.e. wherever it is in transit on the SAN) and when it is at rest on the storage devices.

4.2 Authentication

Authentication can be provided in numerous ways. In order to limit the attacker's ability to enumerate the SAN, choose Fibre Channel switches that require authentication before allowing a connection to a management interface. Authentication should be used to prevent masquerading and Denial-of-Service (DoS) attacks. Switches connect to each other in a SAN via E-ports. Authentication should be performed between switches to prevent the loss of fabric information via an E-port connection to a rogue SAN switch. For architectures requiring the most secure level of security assurance, disable E-port replication (i.e. automatic transfer of fabric information to any connected switch). Any of the following authentication mechanisms may be present in a given piece of equipment. The most secure authentication features that are available should be used.

The FC-SP standard mechanism for switches to authenticate to each other is the Diffie-Hellman Challenge Handshake Authentication Protocol (DH-CHAP). It must be implemented in FC-SP compliant implementations, and it must be configured to function properly within the

SAN architecture. SHA-1 is stronger than MD5, so SHA-1 should be chosen as the DH-CHAP hash algorithm. Additionally, whenever a DH-CHAP challenge is sent, ensure that it is unique.

The Fibre Channel Authentication Protocol (FCAP) and Fibre Channel Password Authentication Protocol (FCPAP) are optional authentication mechanisms that are part of the FC-SP framework. FCAP is a digital certificate-based mechanism. FCPAP is a password-based mechanism. FCAP and FCPAP should be used when available. Vendors might choose to implement an authentication protocol that is not FC-SP compliant. For instance, Brocade offers a proprietary authentication protocol in its secure Fabric OS known as Switch Link Authentication Protocol (SLAP). SLAP is a digital certificate-based mechanism. Vendor proprietary authentication mechanisms should be used when no alternative FC-SP mechanisms are available. If FC-SP and proprietary mechanisms are available, implement the strongest mechanisms.

Authentication of administrative traffic to management ports on SAN equipment is also important. If possible, management LUN should be done out-of-band using an IP management network that has no connectivity to the Internet or other networks. However, if this is not feasible, use the Common Transport (CT) Authentication protocol (which is part of FC-SP) to authenticate in-band (Fibre Channel) network management communications.

4.3 Access Control

A variety of mechanisms exist for providing and supporting access control in SANs. Zoning, LUN masking, and the way in which nodes are identified can all be used to provide access control. Proprietary mechanisms such as Cisco Virtual SANs can be used as well. Other features that should either be used or disabled to provide access control are cut-through switching, physical port locking, and port type locking. Name servers should control access to their information. Each of these access control mechanisms will be described in turn.

4.3.1 Zoning

There are a number of SAN zoning mechanisms available to provide access control for data. Some are more secure than others: 1) Port-based hard zoning, 2) port-based soft zoning, 3) port WWN-based hard zoning, 4) port WWN-based soft zoning, 5) node WWN-based hard zoning, and 6) node WWN-based soft zoning.

Port-based hard zoning should be used to achieve a high level of access control assurance. Port-based hard zoning counters zone hopping attacks, WWN spoofing, and LUN masking attacks. Port WWN-based hard zoning should be used to achieve a medium-high level of access control assurance. Node WWN-based hard zoning, port-based soft zoning, or port WWN-based soft zoning should be used to provide a medium level of access control assurance. Node WWN-based soft zoning is an insecure solution that should not be used. Zoning changes should be forced to take effect immediately.

4.3.2 LUN Masking

Logical Unit Number (LUN) masking is used to specify the visibility of logical units of data to servers. It should be implemented properly to help prevent LUN masking attacks in which attackers would access data that they should not be able to access. The masking mechanism can be implemented at different points in the SAN. Implement LUN masking on the storage devices for the highest level of security assurance. Implement LUN masking on SAN switches for a medium level of security assurance. Do not configure LUN masking at the servers since this is the least secure location for implementing LUN masking. LUN masking software is more vulnerable to attack if it is located on servers rather than the switches or storage devices, since the servers are probably more accessible to attackers than switches and storage devices. The more accessible the LUN masking mechanism is on the network, the more vulnerable the SAN is to attack.

4.3.3 Node Identification

A network node is any entity that is connected to the network and is addressable. There are different ways to address network nodes. Thus, there are different ways to identify nodes, particularly when implementing LUN masking or a zoning mechanism that is WWN-based. These different forms of node identification provide different levels of security. Use World Wide Port Name (WWPN) + World Wide Node Name (WWNN) for authorization when possible to identify nodes for LUN masking and WWN zoning. This is the most secure form of node identification and will help to prevent LUN masking attacks. Port WWN alone will provide less security assurance, if you can verify with the vendor or by some other means that the software only checks port WWN rather than checking either port or node WWN. Node WWN alone should never be used since it is easily spoofed and therefore insecure.

4.3.4 Proprietary Access Control – Cisco Virtual SAN (VSAN)

Use proprietary access controls when they are available to help secure the SAN, e.g. Cisco Virtual SANs (VSANs), which are similar to VLANs. When properly configured, VSANs can help mitigate certain attacks, including zone hopping, WWN spoofing, and LUN masking attacks. Care should be taken when determining what type of VSAN to implement. Static VSANs are configured according to physical switch port numbers, and are more secure than dynamic VSANs, which are configured based on port WWN or node WWN. Avoid dynamic VSANs if possible, but if they must be used, prefer port WWN-based dynamic VSANs.

4.3.5 Cut-through Switching, Physical Port Locking, and Port Type Locking

Access Control can also be provided by disabling or using different SAN switch features such as cut-through switching, physical port locking, and port type locking. These features specify both physical switch port and traffic switching controls. Cut-through switching is a method of switching traffic that offers performance gains, but at the cost of reduced security. If cut-through switching is an option on a SAN switch, disable it.

Physical port locking, also referred to as port binding, is similar to port security on Cisco LAN switches, and should be used when available. It associates a particular WWN with a specific physical port. It should be used for all connected ports on a SAN switch (i.e. not just some connected ports).

Port type locking allows the SAN administrator to specify what type of device (e.g. switch, HBA) should be connected to each port on the switch by locking ports to port types (e.g.

E-port, F-port). All major Fibre Channel switch vendors support port type locking, so it should be used to help mitigate E-port replication attacks.

4.3.6 Name Server

Access Control techniques apply to name server practices as well. Each SAN switch has a name server, and name server information is synchronized among the switches in a SAN fabric. The purpose of the name server is to provide SAN nodes with addresses of other nodes within the fabric. Name server replies should only be sent to requests from authorized nodes in a given zone. This will help to prevent enumeration, name server corruption, and zone hopping attacks.

4.4 Sample SAN Security Architecture

A SAN architecture that implements security mechanisms is shown in Figure 2. Management is performed using secure protocols. A router with a three-legged firewall is positioned between the end-user network, the DMZ network, and the Internet. NIDS are strategically positioned around the router/firewall. SAN switch-to-switch communication is authenticated using DH-CHAP and encrypted using an appropriate algorithm. Port WWN + Node WWN–based LUN masking is performed at the two disk storage devices. Backups are performed to a tape device. Confidentiality of data in transit between a Fibre Channel switch and connected storage devices is protected with encryption performed by an encryption device connected to a port on the Fibre Channel switch. Only one encryption device is shown in the diagram due to space limitations, but each switch should have an associated encryption device. Data is also replicated to a disaster recovery network physically located off-site. The data is sent to the disaster recovery site encrypted as well. The key used to decrypt this data at the disaster recovery site should be stored in a secure location off of the main SAN site in case a disaster affects the SAN.

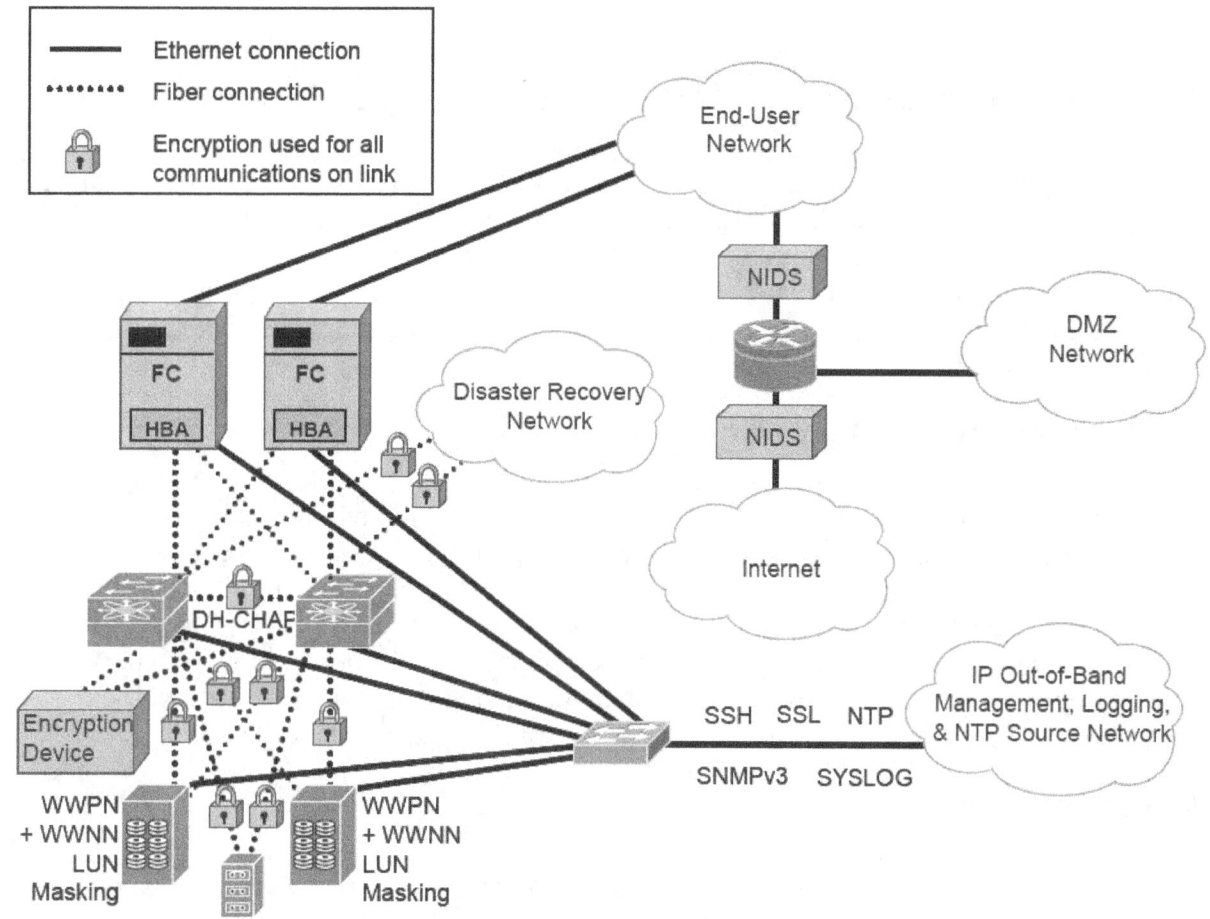

Figure 2: SAN Architecture with Added Security

5. Internet Small Computer Systems Interface (iSCSI) Security

Securing the Internet Small Computer Systems Interface (iSCSI) environment requires proper employment of all general storage network best practices, some NAS and SAN security mechanisms (e.g. zoning, LUN masking), and other security mechanisms specific to the iSCSI environment. Integrity, confidentiality, and authentication can be achieved by using the following mechanisms. By implementing these mechanisms, a reasonable level of security assurance can be gained.

5.1 Confidentiality and Integrity

Confidentiality and integrity can be provided to the iSCSI environment by the use of two mechanisms: IPSec ESP and Cyclic Redundancy Check (CRC) checksums. Use IPSec ESP between iSCSI devices that communicate via IP to provide data confidentiality. Use Cyclic Redundancy Check (CRC) checksums on each IP packet to provide integrity assurance. The packet recipient calculates a checksum on the received packet and compares it to the checksum that was sent with the packet. Any difference in the compared values indicates a lack of integrity. Enable CRC checksums to cover the entire packet, both the header and the data.

5.2 Authentication

Challenge Handshake Authentication Protocol (CHAP) is a protocol that will allow an iSCSI device to authenticate to another iSCSI device. Although the CHAP protocol has weaknesses, some implementations of CHAP are more secure than others. A best practice is to choose devices that implement a relatively secure implementation of CHAP and enable it for use in the iSCSI architecture.

The following items should be considered before purchasing a CHAP solution to ensure that the implementation is relatively secure. CHAP challenges should not be repeated. A unique challenge should be sent each time. When an iSCSI target storage device sends a challenge, if it receives the same challenge back before getting a correct response, it should ignore and log the challenge.

CHAP can be implemented as either one-way CHAP or as mutual CHAP. Using an iSCSI client and a storage device as an example, one-way CHAP only authenticates the iSCSI client to the storage device. Mutual CHAP authenticates an iSCSI client to a storage device as well as authenticates the storage device to the iSCSI client. Use mutual CHAP authentication for a medium-high level of authentication assurance. One-way CHAP authentication provides a lower level of authentication assurance.

5.3 Internet Storage Name Server (iSNS) Best Practices

An iSCSI environment might optionally employ one or more Internet Storage Name Servers (iSNS). If it does, they should be used as security management and security policy distribution devices between clients and storage devices. Multiple iSNS discovery domains should be created, and whenever a new node connects to the network, it should be placed in an untrusted domain until security mechanisms are applied to the new node.

iSNS communications should be secured. The confidentiality and integrity of unicast messages should be protected using IPSec. Broadcast and multicast communications should be authenticated with a Public Key Infrastructure (PKI).

5.4 Sample iSCSI Security Architecture

An iSCSI architecture that incorporates security mechanisms is shown in Figure 3. Secure protocols are used for management of iSCSI network devices. A router with a three-legged firewall is positioned between the end-user network, the DMZ network, and the Internet. NIDS are strategically positioned around the router/firewall. CHAP is used for mutual authentication between iSCSI initiators (clients) and iSCSI storage router devices. IPSec ESP is used between iSCSI initiators and storage routers to maintain a level of data confidentiality.

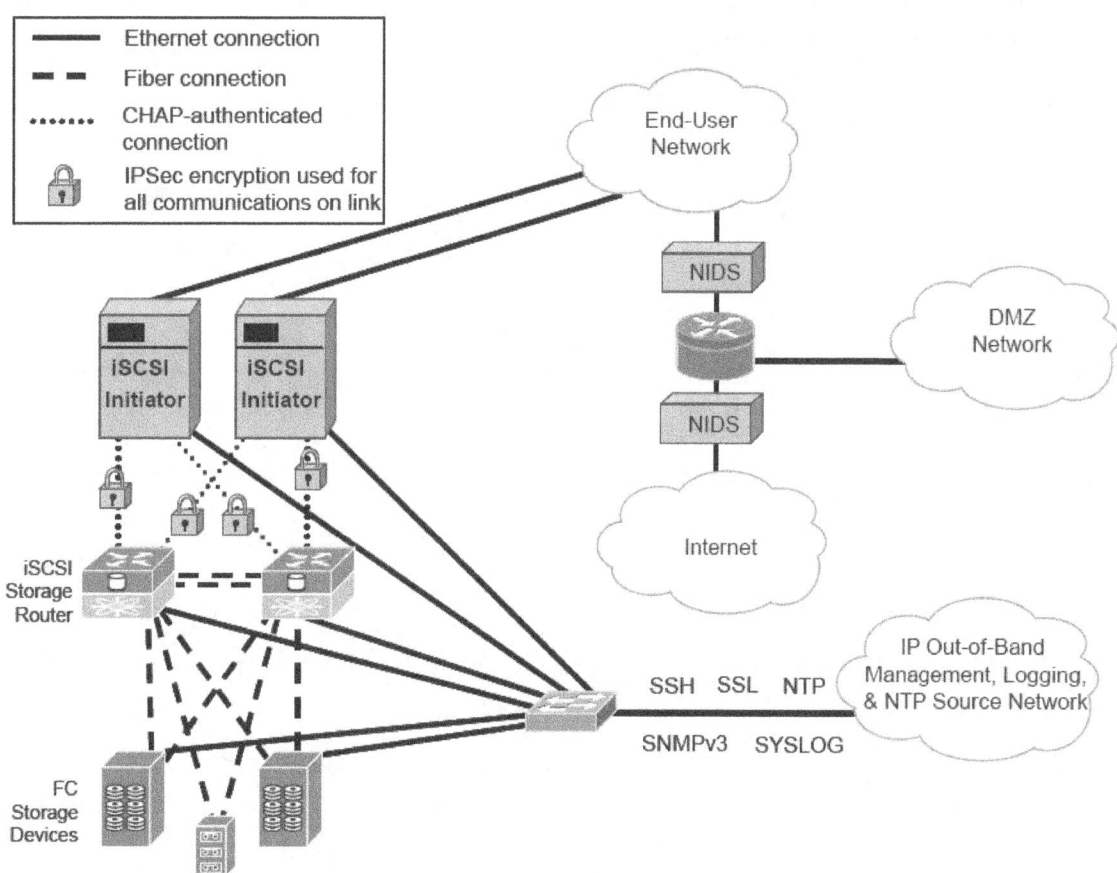

Figure 3: iSCSI Architecture with Added Security

15

6. Conclusions

Best practices for securing storage networks were presented in this document. General storage network security was discussed, followed by a presentation of best practices for three distinct storage technologies: Network Attached Storage (NAS), Storage Area Networks (SAN), and Internet Small Computer Systems Interface (iSCSI). Diagrams were offered that show each of the three types of storage networks with security mechanisms incorporated into the networks.

The best practices outlined in this paper will provide administrators with the information they need to strengthen their storage networks. Using mechanisms that provide authentication, access control, confidentiality, and data integrity will make it harder for attackers to use malicious code to take advantage of functionality errors or protocol faults within the storage networks. Implementing the best practices described in this paper will help protect the content and function of NAS, SAN and iSCSI storage networks and provide a sufficient level of information assurance for most storage architectures.

Appendix 1 - Acronyms

ACL – Access Control List
AES – Advanced Encryption Standard
AH – Authentication Header
ARP – Address Resolution Protocol
CHAP – Challenge Handshake Authentication Protocol
CIFS – Common Internet File System
CRC – Cyclic Redundancy Check
CT – Common Transport
DES – Data Encryption Standard
DH-CHAP – Diffie-Hellman Challenge Handshake Authentication Protocol
DMZ – Demilitarized Zone
DoS – Denial-of-Service
EAL – Evaluation Assurance Level
ESP – Encapsulating Security Payload
FC-SP – Fibre Channel Security Protocols
FCAP – Fibre Channel Authentication Protocol
FCP – Fibre Channel Protocol
FCPAP – Fibre Channel Password Authentication Protocol
FIPS – Federal Information Processing Standards
FTP – File Transfer Protocol
HBA – Host Bus Adapter
HIDS – Host-based Intrusion Detection System
HTTP – Hypertext Transfer Protocol
IDS – Intrusion Detection System
IP – Internet Protocol
IPSec – IP Security
iSCSI – Internet Small Computer Systems Interface
iSNS – Internet Storage Name Server
KDC – Key Distribution Center
LAN – Local Area Network
LM – LAN Manager
LUN – Logical Unit Number
MAC – Media Access Control
MD5 – Message Digest 5
NAS – Network Attached Storage
NDMP – Network Data Management Protocol
NFS – Network File System
NIDS – Network-based Intrusion Detection System
NTLMv1 – New Technology Local Area Network Manager version 1
NTLMv2 – New Technology Local Area Network Manager version 2
NTP – Network Time Protocol
OOB – Out-of-band

OPSEC – Operations Security
OS – Operating System
PKI – Public Key Infrastructure
RBAC – Role-Based Access Control
RSH – Remote Shell
SAN – Storage Area Network
SHA-1 – Secure Hash Algorithm 1
SLAP – Switch Link Authentication Protocol
SNMP – Simple Network Management Protocol
SNMPv1 - Simple Network Management Protocol version 1
SNMPv2 - Simple Network Management Protocol version 2
SNMPv3 - Simple Network Management Protocol version 3
SSH – Secure Shell
SSL – Secure Sockets Layer
STIG – Security Technical Implementation Guide
TCP – Transmission Control Protocol
UPS – Uninterruptible Power Supply
vFiler – Virtual Filer
VLAN – Virtual Local Area Network
VSAN – Virtual Storage Area Network
WWN – World Wide Name
WWNN – World Wide Node Name
WWPN – World Wide Port Name

Appendix 2 – General Storage Network Best Practices Summary

The following table is a quick reference that summarizes the general storage network best practices covered in this document. Section numbers are used to reference each best practice found in the table. Each best practice is associated with the primary security service(s) that it provides. Security services include Confidentiality (C), Integrity (I), Availability (Avail), Access Control (AC), Authentication (Auth), and Attack Detection (AD). In cases where the best practice (see table) contains a numbered list of items, the best practices are listed in order from most secure to least secure.

General Storage Network Best Practice	Security Services Provided
(2.1) Physical Security	AC, Avail, C, I
(2.1) Disable unnecessary ports (physical and logical) and protocols on all storage network devices and management workstations	AC, Avail
(2.1) OPSEC	C
(2.1) Maintain business continuity and disaster recovery plans	Avail
(2.1) Perform backups and securely store backup media; maintain local and offsite copies of operating systems, configurations, application software, and data	Avail
(2.2) Maintain a storage security policy and related documentation	AC, AD, Auth, Avail, C, I
(2.2) Perform a risk analysis before deploying new devices to reassess protection levels	AC, C, I
(2.2) Use devices that have achieved the highest EAL and FIPS certification levels	AC, Auth, Avail, C, I
(2.3) Use UPS, redundancy, and failover mechanisms	Avail
(2.3) Use the strongest encryption and hash algorithms available throughout the storage architecture	C, I
(2.3) Encrypt administration and management communications by using protocols that support cryptography (e.g. SSL, SSH, SNMPv3)	C
(2.4) Appropriately restrict SNMP and administrative traffic via access lists	AC
(2.4) Use SNMPv3 over v1 or v2 if using SNMP	AC, C, I
(2.4) Log SNMP communications	AD

(2.4) Configure strong, unique passwords and strong, unique SNMP community strings, and change passwords regularly	AC
(2.4) Use two or more factor authentication for administrators	Auth

(2.4)
   1. Manage devices locally over serial port
   2. Manage devices OOB remotely using strong encryption (e.g. SSL, SSH)
   3. Manage devices in-band remotely using strong encryption (e.g. SSL, SSH)
	AC, Avail, I

(2.4) Disable insecure protocols such as TELNET, FTP, RSH, and HTTP	AC
(2.4) Use RBAC	AC
(2.4) Close all terminal shell windows and log off of the administrative workstation immediately after performing administrative tasks on SAN devices	AC
(2.4) After using the serial port on a SAN device to manage the device, log out of the SAN device before physically unplugging the cable from the serial port	AC
(2.5) Apply layer two/three security mechanisms (e.g. ACLs, VLANs)	AC, Avail, C, I
(2.5) Monitor for IP spoofing	AD
(2.6) Keep current with virus scanner and anti-spyware updates, and delete unnecessary programs	C, I

(2.6)
   1. Remove debuggers from operational storage network devices
   2. Disable debuggers resident on operational storage network devices
	Avail, C

(2.6) Keep current with patches, and verify patches on a non-operational network before installing them on the operational network	I
(2.6) Obtain software/firmware upgrades from trusted sources, and perform periodic audit	I
(2.7) Log appropriate network and system activities, and write logs to external devices	AD, I
(2.7) Synchronize time using a local OOB time source	AD
(2.7) Deploy NIDS and HIDS	AD
(2.7) Deploy firewalls	AC

Appendix 3 – NAS Best Practices Summary

The following table is a quick reference that summarizes the NAS best practices covered in this document. Section numbers are used to reference each best practice found in the table. Each best practice is associated with the primary security service(s) that it provides. Security services include Confidentiality (C), Integrity (I), Availability (Avail), Access Control (AC), Authentication (Auth), and Attack Detection (AD). In cases where the NAS best practice (see table) contains a numbered list of items, the best practices are listed in order from most secure to least secure.

NAS Best Practice	Security Services Provided
(3.1) Employ IPSec (ESP + AH) between NAS device and each connecting client	C, I
(3.1) Use an in-line encryption device to encrypt data destined for NAS (and tape) devices	C
(3.2) Require authentication if using NDMP	Auth
(3.2) Filter unauthorized devices	AC
(3.3.1) 1. Use separate NAS devices on physically separate networks for physical segmentation 2. Use a Virtual Filer (vFiler) for logical segmentation	AC
(3.3.2) If CIFS is used: 1. Deploy Kerberos; require mutual Kerberos authentication; disable LM, and NTLMv1; monitor for LM, NTLMv1, NTLMv2 traffic 2. Use NTLMv2; disable and monitor for LM, NTLMv1	AD, Auth
(3.3.2) If CIFS is used: Restrict share permissions by users and groups	AC, C
(3.3.3) If NFS is used: Deploy Kerberos; require mutual Kerberos authentication	Auth
(3.3.3) If NFS is used: Log and ignore requests from privileged users originating from unexpected IP addresses	AC, C
(3.3.3) If NFS is used: Treat 'root' requests as being from 'nobody'	AC, C
(3.3.3) If NFS is used: Use export options appropriately	AC, C

(3.3.3) If NFS is used:
  1. Log and ignore 'showmount' requests to NAS devices
  2. Create local hostname aliases; configure exports to aliases only
	AC, C

Appendix 4 – SAN Best Practices Summary

The following table is a quick reference that summarizes each of the SAN best practices covered in this document. Section numbers are used to reference each best practice found in the table. Each best practice is associated with the primary security service(s) that it provides. Security services include Confidentiality (C), Integrity (I), Availability (Avail), Access Control (AC), Authentication (Auth), and Attack Detection (AD). In cases where the SAN best practice (see table) contains a numbered list of items, the best practices are listed in order from most secure to least secure.

SAN Best Practice	Security Services Provided
(4.1) Implement FC-SP ESP	C
(4.1) Encrypt inter-switch communications	C
(4.1) Encrypt data-at-rest on storage devices by using an encryption appliance	C
(4.2) Choose FC switches that require authentication before allowing connections to FC switch management interfaces	Auth
(4.2) Disable E-port replication	C
(4.2) Perform authentication between switches using DH-CHAP (FC-SP standard means of switch authentication)	Auth
(4.2) Ensure unique DH-CHAP challenges are sent each time	Auth
(4.2) Use FCAP	Auth
(4.2) Use FCPAP	Auth
(4.2) Use proprietary authentication protocols such as SLAP	Auth

(4.2)
  1. Perform OOB management from a network that is not connected to any other network
  2. Perform in-band Fibre Channel management using CT authentication
	AC, Avail, C, I

(4.3.1) Implement zones in the most secure way:
  1. Port-based hard zoning
  2. Port WWN-based hard zoning
  3. Node WWN-based hard zoning OR port-based soft zoning OR port WWN-based soft zoning
	AC

(4.3.1) Push zoning changes immediately	AC, I

(4.3.2) Implement LUN masking on:
   1. Storage devices
   2. SAN switches
	AC, C

(4.3.3) Identify nodes for LUN masking and WWN Zoning:
   1. Use WWPN + WWNN
   2. Use WWPN only
	AC

(4.3.4) Use proprietary access controls such as VSANs:
   1. Static VSANs
   2. Port WWN-based dynamic VSANs
	AC

(4.3.5) Disable cut-through switching	I
(4.3.5) Use physical port locking, also known as port binding, for all connected ports on SAN switches	AC
(4.3.5) Use port type locking to specify the type of device that can be connected to each specific port on a SAN switch	AC, C
(4.3.6) Do not reply to SAN switch Name Server requests from unauthorized nodes	C

Appendix 5 – iSCSI Best Practices Summary

The following table is a quick reference that summarizes each of the iSCSI best practices covered in this document. Section numbers are used to reference each best practice found in the table. Each best practice is associated with the primary security service(s) that it provides. Security services include Confidentiality (C), Integrity (I), Availability (Avail), Access Control (AC), Authentication (Auth), and Attack Detection (AD). In cases where the iSCSI best practice (see table) contains a numbered list of items, the best practices are listed in order from most secure to least secure.

iSCSI Best Practice	Security Services Provided
(5.1) Use CRC Checksums	I
(5.1) Use IPSec ESP between iSCSI devices	C
(5.2) Acquire relatively secure CHAP implementations and configure CHAP securely; CHAP challenges should not be repeated; a unique challenge should be sent each time; a challenge received that matches a challenge sent (before receiving a response) should be ignored and logged	Auth
(5.2) 1. Use mutual CHAP authentication between iSCSI devices 2. Use non-mutual CHAP authentication	Auth
(5.3) If using iSNS: Use the iSNS server as a security management and policy distribution service	AC, C, I
(5.3) If using iSNS: Place new nodes in an untrusted domain until security mechanisms are applied	AC
(5.3) If using iSNS: Protect unicast messages with IPSec ESP	C, I
(5.3) If using iSNS: Authenticate broadcast and multicast messages with a PKI	Auth

Appendix 6 - References

[1]   Beauchamp and Judd, Kuo (contributor) 2001. Building SANs with Brocade Fabric
       Switches: How to Design, Implement, and Maintain Storage Area Networks (SANs) with
       Brocade Fabric Switches. Syngress Publishing, Inc.

[2]   Farley, M. 2005. Storage Networking Fundamentals: An Introduction to Storage Devices,
       Subsystems, Applications, Management, and File Systems. Cisco Systems, Inc. (Cisco
       Press)

[3]   Dwivedi, H. 2006. Securing Storage: A Practical Guide to SAN and NAS Security.
       Pearson Education, Inc. (Addison-Wesley)

[4]   Chirillo and Blaul 2003. Storage Security: Protecting SANs, NAS, and DAS. Wiley
       Publishing, Inc.

[5]   Internet Web site: http://whatis.techtargetget.com/definition

[6]   Internet Web site: http://en.wikipedia.org/wiki/ISCSI

[7]   Internet Web Site:
       http://www.viglen.co.uk/storagegroup/pdfs/Microsoft_Deploying_iSCSI_SAN-
       July2004.pdf

[8]   Internet Web Site:
       http://www.snia.org/ssif/practices/

[9]   Storage Networking Industry Association 2005. Audit Logging for Storage: A SNIA
       Security White Paper.

[10]   Internet Web Site: http://en.wikipedia.org/wiki/Role-Based_Access_Control

[11]   Internet Web Site: http://www.sansecurity.com/san-security-faq.shtml

[12]   Cisco Storage Networking Fundamentals for the End User, Student Guide, Version 2.0

[13]   SNIA IP Storage Forum End User Education CD-ROM

[14]   SNIA Resources CD-ROM April 2007

[15]   Storage Networking Industry Association 2006. The Dictionary of Storage Networking
       Terminology

www.ingramcontent.com/pod-product-compliance
Lightning Source LLC
Chambersburg PA
CBHW080800290526
45790CB00008B/3531